PYTHON

For Mere Mortals

*Learn Python by building a simple project -- even
if you're not a programmer*

Nick Chase

For my darling wife Sarah Jane, who is
so much more than a mere mortal

Table of Contents

Acknowledgements

I'd like to take a moment to thank everyone who helped with the writing and editing of this book, including John Jainschigg, David Fishman, Simon Kariuki, and especially Bruce Basil Matthews, who helped point out some places that weren't quite clear and suggested ways to clear up the confusion.

Who this book is for

As a general rule, I tend to avoid learning a new programming language until I'm forced to because I need it for a particular project. The upside of this is that I don't waste my time on a language that may not be useful to me. The downside is that I often spend a lot of time being intimidated by a language that a lot of other people are using.

Most recently, that was what happened with Python, a powerful interpreted, object-oriented scripting language behind sites such as Google, YouTube, Yahoo and Quora.

I'd managed to get by without getting into its strictly indexed goodness (even after years of working in the OpenStack market) until realizing it was the best way for me to use Tensorflow to learn machine learning.

Fortunately, Python is really pretty easy to learn and use. In this book we're going to create a sample application that shows you how to:

- Take info from the command line
- Output text

- Use a for-loop
- Read a file
- Write to a file
- Create a function
- Import a library

To do that, we'll look at an old standby favorite app of mine: the Really Simple Syndication (RSS) reader, which enables you to read web news feeds, podcast feeds, and so on.

This book is for anyone who wants to get started with Python. It will be easier if you have programming experience, but it's not essential: everything you need to get started is right here. The main thing is to take it slowly and concentrate on one step at a time.

If you have questions, join me at
http://www.technologyformeremortals.com/python-book
and I'll do my best to help you out. (You can also register to get free updates of this book as I add new features.)

Setting up

If you're using Linux you should already have Python installed, though it may be an older version. You can also download binaries for Linux and various operating systems such as Windows and Mac from https://www.python.org/.

There are literally dozens of different ways to install Python. For example, if you're using Ubuntu, rather than directly downloading binaries, you could simply type:

```
sudo apt-get update
sudo apt-get install python3
```

If you're using Windows or MacOS, you can download the proper installer and run it just like any other installer.

Either way, the important thing is to ensure that you're using a version of Python 3 so that you can follow along with the code examples. Python 2 is still available, but there are important syntax changes between the two.

To ensure you're using the right version, type:

```
python --version
```

Creating and running a basic Python script

Let's start out by doing something extremely simple. The traditional "starting point" is a "Hello world" script, so let's start there. All we want to do is print some text, which is pretty much as simple as it seems:

1) Create a new text file and name it python4mm.py.
2) Add the following code:

```
print ("Hello, world!")
```

3) Save the file and run the script by typing

```
python3 ./python4mm.py
```

on the command line. If you get output of

```
Hello, world!
```

then you know everything is working perfectly.

Now, that was a pretty simple task, but we can already learn a whole lot from it. Let's take a look at the syntax here:

```
print ("Hello world!")
```

Here's what we know so far, just from this one line script:

1) There aren't any line numbers.
2) When we send data to a function (such as `print()`) we enclose it in parentheses.
3) Strings, or bits of text, get enclosed in quotation marks. (It's a style choice; single quotes (') would have worked too.)
4) There are no semi-colons or other line-ending marks.
5) Python as an interpreted language, so we don't have to compile the script.
6) We don't have to import anything to do basic operations.

That's a good start from just one line! Now let's start actually doing something and see what else we can learn.

Working with variables

Now let's look at giving ourselves a little more functionality. We can start by creating and outputting a variable, or a placeholder for a piece of information. Go back to your `python4mm.py` file and add:

```
print ("Hello world!")

feed_url = "http://www.mirantis.com/feed/"
print ("We're going to output the feed at: "
+ feed_url)
```

Now if you save and run the file, you'll get additional output:

```
Hello, world!
We're going to output the feed at:
http://www.mirantis.com/feed/
```

This snippet shows us a few more things:

1) Variables, or placeholders for information, are just names. They don't have a dollar sign, or anything else that distinguishes them. If it's a word and it's

not a "reserved" word such as "print", it's going to be treated as a variable.

2) We can combine strings using the plus sign (+). (There are other ways to do it, but we're starting small.)

3) Each print statement is going to output on its own line, even though we didn't tell it to.

So far we've been dealing only with built-in functions. Sometimes, though, Python itself doesn't give you what you need, and you need to get more help. In the next step, we'll do that by importing a package.

The sample project

In our example, we're going to use a package called feedparser, which is designed to read RSS and Atom feeds. These feeds are carefully constructed text that provides information on articles that have been published by a site so that you can easily "syndicate" them. It's also used to publish information about podcasts so podcast apps can find them.

The nice thing about RSS feeds is that you don't need to worry about deciphering the actual content. For example, our sample feed looks something like this. Notice that it's formatted in a predictable way so a program (such as `feedparser`) can easily extract the information:

```
<?xml version="1.0" encoding="UTF-8"?>
<rss version="2.0"
xmlns:dc="http://purl.org/dc/elements/1.1/"
>
<channel>
    <title>Mirantis | Pure Play Open
Cloud</title>
    <link>https://www.mirantis.com</link>
```

```xml
<description>Pure Play Open
Cloud</description>
    <lastBuildDate>Mon, 26 Feb 2018
20:21:42</lastBuildDate>
    <language>en-US</language>

    <item>
        <title>What is Hyperconverged
Infrastructure?/title>

<link>https://www.mirantis.com/blog/what-is
-hyperconverged
-infrastructure-hci-and-when-should-i-use-i
t-pros-and-cons-of-hci-and-traditional-arch
itecture/</link>

<comments>https://www.mirantis.com/blog/wha
t-is-
hyperconverged-infrastructure-hci-and-when-
should-i-use-it-pros-and-cons-of-hci-and-tr
aditional-architecture/#respond</comments>
        <pubDate>Sun, 11 Feb 2018 01:07:50
+0000</pubDate>
        <category>Blog</category>
        <category>HCI</category>
        <category>hyperconverged</category>
        <guid isPermaLink="false"

>https://www.mirantis.com/?p=664205</guid>
        <description>There are good reasons
to use Hyperconverged Infrastructure, but
there are also downsides you need to take
into consideration.</description>
```

```
      </item>
      <item>
          <title>The Intelligent Delivery
Manifesto</title>

<link>https://www.mirantis.com/blog/intelli
gent-delivery- manifesto/</link>

<comments>https://www.mirantis.com/blog/int
elligent-deliver
y-manifesto/#respond</comments>
          <pubDate>Mon, 15 Jan 2018 15:59:14
+0000</pubDate>
          <category>Blog</category>
          <category>icd></category>
          <category>intelligent continuous
delivery</category>
          <guid isPermaLink="false"

>https://www.mirantis.com/?p=663708</guid>
          <description>All of the pieces
necessary to create Intelligent Delivery
already exist, from Infrastructure as Code
to multi-cloud to machine learning. Now we
need to combine them into a single
methodology.</description>
      </item>
          ...
</channel>
</rss>
```

You can see this data in its full glory for yourself if you point
your browser to https://www.mirantis.com/feed/. It's in a

format called XML, which means that the data is surrounded by tags such as `<category></category>` or `<description></description>`, and that it can be "nested", with one or more tags completely enclosed by another pair of tags. For example, the `<item></item>` tags have several nested tags within them, such as `<title></title>`, `<link></link>`, and so on.

In our simple project, we're going to use `feedparser` to retrieve this data, then loop through each item and print out the `title`. Then we'll write a function that creates the output, and finally, learn how to take the feed URL from the command line.

When we're finished, we'll have a basic application that can be used to read RSS feeds.

Let's start with `feedparser` itself.

Importing Python libraries

Like virtually all programming languages, Python makes it possible to create modules, or libraries, that can be imported into other programs. Sometimes these libraries are included with Python, sometimes you have to install them separately.

In this case, `feedparser` is included with Python, so that makes it simple. All we need to do is add an `import` statement to the top of `python4mm.py`:

```
import feedparser

print ("Hello, world!")

feed_url = "http://www.mirantis.com/feed/"
print ("We're going to output the feed at:
" + feed_url)
```

You can run the script at this point, but you won't see anything different because we didn't make feedparser actually DO anything. To do that, we need to actually parse the feed:

```
import feedparser

print ("Hello, world!")

feed_url = "http://www.mirantis.com/feed/"
print ("We're going to output the feed at:
" + feed_url)

the_feed_object = feedparser.parse(feed_url)
```

OK, so let's see what we've got here. We're creating a variable called `the_feed_object`, and what we're assigning to that variable is the output of `feedparser`'s `parse()` function. The `parse()` function retrieves the text and parses it out into specific pieces of information, then puts those pieces of information into particular slots, or "attributes", of `the_feed_object`.

If you wanted to, you could just print out the actual feed object using

```
print (the_feed_object)
```

But the results are pretty unfriendly:

```
We're going to output the feed at: http://www.mirantis.com/feed/
nick@machinelearning:~/Documents/python4mm$ python3 python4mm.py
Hello, world!
We're going to output the feed at: http://www.mirantis.com/feed/
{'namespaces': {'': 'http://www.w3.org/2005/Atom', 'wfw': 'http://wellformedweb.
org/CommentAPI/', 'content': 'http://purl.org/rss/1.0/modules/content/', 'dc': '
http://purl.org/dc/elements/1.1/', 'sy': 'http://purl.org/rss/1.0/modules/syndic
ation/', 'slash': 'http://purl.org/rss/1.0/modules/slash/'}, 'updated': 'Mon, 26
 Feb 2018 20:44:29 GMT', 'version': 'rss20', 'feed': {'links': [{'type': 'applic
ation/rss+xml', 'href': 'https://www.mirantis.com/feed/', 'rel': 'self'}, {'type
': 'text/html', 'href': 'https://www.mirantis.com', 'rel': 'alternate'}], 'subti
tle_detail': {'language': None, 'type': 'text/html', 'base': 'https://www.mirant
is.com/feed/', 'value': 'Pure Play Open Cloud'}, 'sy_updatefrequency': '1', 'tit
le': 'Mirantis | Pure Play Open Cloud', 'title_detail': {'language': None, 'type
': 'text/plain', 'base': 'https://www.mirantis.com/feed/', 'value': 'Mirantis |
Pure Play Open Cloud'}, 'subtitle': 'Pure Play Open Cloud', 'updated': 'Mon, 26
Feb 2018 20:44:29 +0000', 'updated_parsed': time.struct_time(tm_year=2018, tm_mo
n=2, tm_mday=26, tm_hour=20, tm_min=44, tm_sec=29, tm_wday=0, tm_yday=57, tm_isd
st=0), 'sy_updateperiod': 'hourly', 'link': 'https://www.mirantis.com', 'languag
e': 'en-US'}, 'etag': '"463be6fb7b223c1c3607bb05e358af1e"', 'encoding': 'UTF-8',
 'bozo': 0, 'status': 301, 'updated_parsed': time.struct_time(tm_year=2018, tm_m
on=2, tm_mday=26, tm_hour=20, tm_min=44, tm_sec=29, tm_wday=0, tm_yday=57, tm_is
dst=0), 'href': 'https://www.mirantis.com/feed/', 'headers': {'X-Nginx-Cache':
MISS', 'X-Content-Type-Options': 'nosniff', 'X-CDN': 'Incapsula', 'Date': 'Mon,
```

Instead, let's look at individual attributes. One of those attributes is the feed itself, which we can get if we do:

```
print (the_feed_object.feed)
```

If we run that we still get a blob of text, but if we clean it up (http://jsonlint.org is great for this) we can see that there's at least some kind of order to it:

```
{
    'link': 'https://www.mirantis.com',
    'sy_updatefrequency': '1',
    'sy_updateperiod': 'hourly',
    'title_detail': {
        'type': 'text/plain',
        'value': 'Mirantis | Pure Play Open
Cloud',
        'base':
'https://www.mirantis.com/feed/',
        'language': None
```

```
    },
    'subtitle': 'Pure Play Open Cloud',
    'title': 'Mirantis | Pure Play Open
Cloud',
    'updated': 'Mon, 26 Feb 2018 20:44:29',
    'subtitle_detail': {
        'type': 'text/html',
        'value': 'Pure Play Open Cloud',
        'base':
'https://www.mirantis.com/feed/',
        'language': None
    },
    'links': [{
        'type': 'application/rss+xml',
        'rel': 'self',
        'href':
'https://www.mirantis.com/feed/'
    }, {
        'type': 'text/html',
        'rel': 'alternate',
        'href': 'https://www.mirantis.com'
    }],
    'updated_parsed':
time.struct_time(tm_year = 2018, tm_mon =
2, tm_mday = 26, tm_hour = 20, tm_min = 44,
tm_sec = 29, tm_wday = 0, tm_yday = 57,
tm_isdst = 0),
    'language': 'en-US'
}
```

This text is in a form called JavaScript Object Notation, or JSON. It's got the same structure as the XML we saw earlier, but rather than tags it uses a name: value notation, with curly braces ({ }) and brackets ([ ]) to group attributes together.

Now we can drill down a little further and grab, say, the title and the last time the feed was updated:

```
...
the_feed_object =
feedparser.parse(feed_url)

print (the_feed_object.feed.title + " was
last updated " +
the_feed_object.feed.updated)
```

As you can see from this example, we're going from the_feed_object to its feed attribute (which is also an object) to feed's title and updated attributes. If we run the script, we can see the results:

```
Hello, world!
We're going to output the feed at:
http://www.mirantis.com/feed/
Mirantis | Pure Play Open Cloud was last
updated Mon, 26 Feb 2018 20:44:29
```

Great! Of course this isn't particularly useful if we can't get the actual articles, so let's look at that next.

Working with Python lists (NOT arrays)

One very common structure in Python is the list, which is like a JavaScript array, in that it's a numbered sequence of n objects, numbered 0 through (n-1). So a 10 item list would be numbered 0 through 9. Python does have another type of structure called an array that acts in a similar way, but it can only hold objects of a single type; we're only going to talk about lists for now.

For example, we might have a list of dogs:

```
dogs = ["Razzle Dazzle", "Johnny", "Holly"]
```

We could then access items by their number, or index. For example, if we were to say:

```
print (dogs[2])
```

we would get the third item (remember, the first item is number 0), so the output would be:

```
Holly
```

We can also do the opposite, creating a list and then populating it by number. So we could accomplish the same thing like this:

```
dogs = []
dogs[0] = "Razzle Dazzle"
dogs[1] = "Johnny"
dogs[2] = "Holly"
```

In the case of our example, the entries for each `feed` are in the `entries` list:

```
...
print (the_feed_object.feed.title + " was
last updated " +
the_feed_object.feed.updated)

items = the_feed_object.entries
number_of_items = len(items)

print ("There are {a} items.".format(a =
number_of_items))
```

So let's look at what we have here. First off, we're retrieving the list of entries, then we're finding out how many items there are by getting the length of that list using the `len()` function.

Then we're outputting the length, but we're doing it by inserting it into the middle of the string using the `format()` function. If this is confusing, don't stress over it; it's just the way that we're getting around the fact that Python can't add a string and a number together. Essentially we're using the curly braces (`{}`) to create a placeholder, called `a` in this case, then we're using the string's `format()` function to assign a value to `a`. This is pretty handy, because we can assign any number of placeholders this way.

Now if we run the script...

```
Hello, world!
We're going to output the feed at:
http://www.mirantis.com/feed/
Mirantis | Pure Play Open Cloud was last
updated Tue, 27 Feb 2018 01:54:51
There are 10 items.
```

Excellent. Just like before, we can access a specific item...

```
print (items[2])
```

In this case, we'll print the third item, but instead of a string, it's an object:

```
Hello, world!
We're going to output the feed at: http://www.mirantis.com/feed/
Mirantis | Pure Play Open Cloud was last updated Tue, 27 Feb 2018 01:54:51 +0000
There are 10 items.
{'summary': '<p>The post <a href="https://www.mirantis.com/webinars/how-massive-
organizations-keep-from-losing-their-clouds-their-data-and-their-sanity/" rel="n
ofollow">How massive organizations keep from losing their clouds, their data, an
d their sanity</a> appeared first on <a href="https://www.mirantis.com" rel="nof
ollow">Mirantis | Pure Play Open Cloud</a>.</p>\n<p>The post <a href="https://ww
w.mirantis.com/webinars/how-massive-organizations-keep-from-losing-their-clouds-
their-data-and-their-sanity/" rel="nofollow">How massive organizations keep from
 losing their clouds, their data, and their sanity</a> appeared first on <a href
="https://www.mirantis.com" rel="nofollow">Mirantis | Pure Play Open Cloud</a>.<
/p>', 'published': 'Mon, 29 Jan 2018 20:37:10 +0000', 'content': [{'base': 'http
s://www.mirantis.com/feed/', 'language': None, 'value': '<p>The post <a href="ht
tps://www.mirantis.com/webinars/how-massive-organizations-keep-from-losing-their
-clouds-their-data-and-their-sanity/" rel="nofollow">How massive organizations k
eep from losing their clouds, their data, and their sanity</a> appeared first on
 <a href="https://www.mirantis.com" rel="nofollow">Mirantis | Pure Play Open Clo
ud</a>.</p>\n<p>The post <a href="https://www.mirantis.com/webinars/how-massive-
organizations-keep-from-losing-their-clouds-their-data-and-their-sanity/" rel="n
ofollow">How massive organizations keep from losing their clouds, their data, an
d their sanity</a> appeared first on <a href="https://www.mirantis.com" rel="nof
ollow">Mirantis | Pure Play Open Cloud</a>.</p>', 'type': 'text/html'}], 'link':
```

That's not very convenient, so let's go ahead and pull out the title:

```
print(items[2].title)
```

Now we get something useful:

```
How massive organizations keep from losing
their clouds, their data, and their sanity
```

Next let's look at looping through all of these items.

Looping in Python (with numbers)

We have several options for looping in Python. The simplest way is to use the numbers, or indexes, of the entries. For example, we can create a loop that executes specific steps as long as we haven't reached the end of the list:

```
...
items = the_feed_object.entries
number_of_items = len(items)

print ("There are {a} items.".format(a =
number_of_items))

this_item = 0
while (this_item < number_of_items) :
    print (this_item)
    print (items[this_item].title)
    this_item = this_item + 1
```

Let's look at what's happening here. We create a new variable called `this_item` and initialize it with the first value, which is `0`. Then we create a loop that we want to run while `this_item` is less than the `number_of_items`. (Since we're starting at 0, if there are 10 items we want to stop at 9.)

Now, a couple of things you should know about this example:

1) The colon (:) at the end of the first line indicates that we're about to start a new block.
2) The block is indicated by the indented lines.
3) INDENTING IS CRUCIAL in Python; it's how Python understands what goes with what. Some editing tools will point out errors in indenting, but regardless of what you use to create your scripts, make sure your indenting is consistent.
4) Use (a consistent number of) spaces to indent, never tabs.
5) Don't forget to increment your counter, or your loop will run forever (or until you press CTRL-C to stop it).

So if we run this, we can see that we loop through each item until we get to the end:

```
0
What's New In Kubernetes 1.10
1
What is Hyperconverged Infrastructure (HCI) and when should I use it? Pros and c
ons of HCI and traditional architecture
2
How massive organizations keep from losing their clouds, their data, and their s
anity
3
Adrian Ionel returns to CEO role at Mirantis as the company continues to expand
beyond OpenStack
4
Co-Founder Adrian Ionel Returns to Mirantis to Lead Company Beyond Private Cloud
5
KQueen: The Open Source Multi-cloud Kubernetes Cluster Manager
6
The Intelligent Delivery Manifesto
7
Containers will Drive Massive Shift in How Companies do Business
8
OpenStack Summit Vancouver
9
KubeCon and CloudNativeCon Europe 2018
nick@machinelearning:~/Documents/python4mm$
```

We can also use a `for-loop` to go through the list by indexes:

```
this_item = 0
for this_item in range(0, number_of_items)
    :
        print (this_item)
        print (items[this_item].title)
```

Some things we can learn from this example:

1) The `range()` function is giving us a sequence of numbers from 0 to `(number_of_items-1)`, so the output is the same as the previous example.
2) With a `for-loop`, we don't have to increment `this_item` manually -- which is convenient, because you will almost invariably forget to do this the first time you run through a `while()` loop.

Looping through indexes is convenient, but it's not the only way to go through a list. Next we'll look at looping through the list directly.

Looping in Python (with objects)

So far we've been counting on knowing how many items there were so that we could specifically loop through that many of them. Sometimes, though, we don't have that option. In those cases, we can loop through the objects specifically, and Python will just stop when it gets to the end. For example:

```
...
print ("There are {a} items.".format(a =
number_of_items))

for this_item in items :
        print (this_item.title)
```

Now, this is a little different from our previous example. Specifically:

1) We don't have to find out how many items there are.
2) In this case, this_item does NOT represent the number of the item, but the actual item itself. Notice that rather than

```
items[this_item].title
```

we're using

```
this_item.title
```

directly. This is because each time Python goes
through the loop, it places the next item into
`this_item`. In other words, this_item becomes a
pointer to the memory position in the stack holding
`items`.

3) We don't have to go through the extra step of locating
   the item, which means that we don't have to have an
   index for it.

If we run the script now, we can see we still get the title:

```
nick@machinelearning:~/Documents/python4mm$ python3 python4mm.py
Hello, world!
We're going to output the feed at: http://www.mirantis.com/feed/
Mirantis | Pure Play Open Cloud was last updated Tue, 27 Feb 2018 23:51:06 +0000
There are 10 items.
What's New In Kubernetes 1.10
What is Hyperconverged Infrastructure (HCI) and when should I use it? Pros and c
ons of HCI and traditional architecture
How massive organizations keep from losing their clouds, their data, and their s
anity
Adrian Ionel returns to CEO role at Mirantis as the company continues to expand
beyond OpenStack
Co-Founder Adrian Ionel Returns to Mirantis to Lead Company Beyond Private Cloud
KQueen: The Open Source Multi-cloud Kubernetes Cluster Manager
The Intelligent Delivery Manifesto
Containers will Drive Massive Shift in How Companies do Business
OpenStack Summit Vancouver
KubeCon and CloudNativeCon Europe 2018
nick@machinelearning:~/Documents/python4mm$
```

Now let's look at encapsulating things a little more.

Python functions

If you're going to create programs that are maintainable, you're going to have to break them up into pieces that you can call from multiple locations. These are called functions, and they let you change functionality in one place and have that change take effect wherever the function is used.

In our case, we're going to create a function that outputs the title of each feed. The syntax is similar to the syntax for a loop:

```python
import feedparser

def print_item_info (target_item) :
        print (target_item.title)

print ("Hello, world!")

...

for this_item in items :
        print_item_info (this_item)
```

So a couple of things to keep in mind:

1) You must declare the function before you reference it so the interpreter knows what it is, but other than that it doesn't matter where you put it in the file. That said, it's common to declare everything at the top of the file, then provide the logic using all of those entities.
2) A function starts with def, then the function name, then any input parameters, then a colon.
3) Just like with our loops, the body of the function is defined by the indent.

This seems like a simple example that didn't warrant a function, and maybe it is, but having the output in a function makes it that much easier for us to change the output without affecting the rest of the program:

```
import feedparser

def print_item_info (target_item):
        print (target_item.title + "(" +
target_item.link + ")")

print ("Hello, world!")
...
```

If we run it we can see the new output:

```
perconverged-infrastructure-hci-and-when-should-i-use-it-pros-and-cons-of-hci-an
d-traditional-architecture/)
How massive organizations keep from losing their clouds, their data, and their s
anity(https://www.mirantis.com/webinars/how-massive-organizations-keep-from-losi
ng-their-clouds-their-data-and-their-sanity/)
Adrian Ionel returns to CEO role at Mirantis as the company continues to expand
beyond OpenStack(https://www.mirantis.com/company/press-center/in-the-media/adri
an-ionel-returns-to-ceo-role-at-mirantis-as-the-company-continues-to-expand-beyo
nd-openstack/)
Co-Founder Adrian Ionel Returns to Mirantis to Lead Company Beyond Private Cloud
(https://www.mirantis.com/company/press-center/company-news/co-founder-adrian-io
nel-returns-to-mirantis-to-lead-company-beyond-private-cloud/)
KQueen: The Open Source Multi-cloud Kubernetes Cluster Manager(https://www.miran
tis.com/blog/kqueen-open-source-multi-cloud-k8s-cluster-manager/)
The Intelligent Delivery Manifesto(https://www.mirantis.com/blog/intelligent-del
ivery-manifesto/)
Containers will Drive Massive Shift in How Companies do Business(https://www.mir
antis.com/company/press-center/in-the-media/containers-will-drive-massive-shift-
in-how-companies-do-business/)
OpenStack Summit Vancouver(https://www.mirantis.com/event/openstack-summit-vanco
uver/)
KubeCon and CloudNativeCon Europe 2018(https://www.mirantis.com/event/kubecon-an
d-cloudnativecon-europe-2018/)
nick@machinelearning:~/Documents/python4mm$
```

So we've got a good basis at this point. We know how to loop
through the items in the feed, and we've created a function
we can use to control the information we're outputting.

But what if we wanted to be more flexible about what feed
we're actually reading?

Reading information from the command line

So far we have one feed that we specified in the body of the script. But what if we wanted to take that information from the command line? Fortunately that's not too difficult:

```python
import feedparser
import sys

print ("Command line is : " + str(sys.argv))

def print_item_info (target_item):
        print (target_item.title + "(" +
target_item.link + ")")
    ...
```

Now let's run the script, but this time, let's add the URL for another feed:

```
$ python3 ./python4mm.py
https://istio.io/feed.xml
Command line is : ['python4mm.py',
'https://istio.io/feed.xml']
```

...

So as you can see, `sys.argv` is a list of all of the items on the command line, starting with the script name itself. So if we wanted to retrieve the feed from the command line, we'd do it by pulling it out of `sys.argv`:

```
import feedparser
import sys

print ("Command line is : " +
str(sys.argv))

def print_item_info (target_item):
        print (target_item.title + "(" +
target_item.link + ")")

print ("Hello, world!")

feed_url = sys.argv[1]

print ("We're going to output the feed at:
" + feed_url)
...
```

Remember, lists are zero-based, so to get the second item, we want item number 1. You could also add additional items to the command line and retrieve them by their position.

Now if we run it again with the same input, we'll see the Istio feed rather than the Mirantis feed:

```
nick@machinelearning:~/Documents/python4mm$ python3 python4mm.py https://istio.i
o/feed.xml
Command line is : ['python4mm.py', 'https://istio.io/feed.xml']
Hello, world!
We're going to output the feed at: https://istio.io/feed.xml
Istio Blog was last updated 2018-03-07T17:31:10+00:00
There are 10 items.
Introducing Istio(https://istio.io/blog/2017/0.1-announcement.html)
Using Istio to Improve End-to-End Security(https://istio.io/blog/2017/0.1-auth.h
tml)
Canary Deployments using Istio(https://istio.io/blog/2017/0.1-canary.html)
Using Network Policy with Istio(https://istio.io/blog/2017/0.1-using-network-pol
icy.html)
Announcing Istio 0.2(https://istio.io/blog/2017/0.2-announcement.html)
Mixer Adapter Model(https://istio.io/blog/2017/adapter-model.html)
Mixer and the SPOF Myth(https://istio.io/blog/2017/mixer-spof-myth.html)
Consuming External Web Services(https://istio.io/blog/2018/egress-https.html)
Consuming External TCP Services(https://istio.io/blog/2018/egress-tcp.html)
Traffic mirroring with Istio for testing in production(https://istio.io/blog/201
8/traffic-mirroring.html)
nick@machinelearning:~/Documents/python4mm$
```

There's one way we can make this even more convenient: reading the feeds from a file.

Reading from a file with Python

It's great that we can retrieve the feed URL from the command line. We could even retrieve multiple URLs if we wanted to. But putting in a bunch of them is going to be a pain. Let's add them to an external text file instead.

The simplest way is to add our feed URLs to a text file, with one per line:

```
https://forums.manning.com/rss/forumTopics/
624.page
https://istio.io/feed.xml
https://www.mirantis.com/feed/
```

We'll save that as a text file called `feeds.txt` in the same directory as `python4mm.py`. Now we can go ahead and retrieve the content:

```
...
print ("Hello, world!")

feed_file = open("feeds.txt", "r")
for this_feed in feed_file:
```

```
    print(this_feed, end="")

  print("\n\n\n")
  feed_file.close()
  . . .
```

First we're creating the file object, `feed_file`, by opening the `feeds.txt` file as a "read only" object (`"r"`). Then we're looping through each line in the file and printing out the feed URL. We'll tell the `print()` function not to put each output on a new line by specifying the end character as " " rather than the default newline character (`"\n"`), because the line itself has its own line feed attached. We'll also add three newline characters to separate this introductory information from the rest of the output.

Now we can run the script without providing the feed URL:

```
nick@machinelearning:~/Documents/python4mm$ python3 python4mm.py
Command line is : ['python4mm.py']
Hello, world!
https://forums.manning.com/rss/forumTopics/624.page
https://istio.io/feed.xml
https://www.mirantis.com/feed/


Traceback (most recent call last):
  File "python4mm.py", line 17, in <module>
    feed_url = sys.argv[1]
IndexError: list index out of range
nick@machinelearning:~/Documents/python4mm$
```

Notice that since we didn't provide a URL on the command line, we had only one item in the `sys.argv` list, so when we tried to call `sys.argv[1]` we got an error.

No matter, we're going to use the URLs from the file anyway:

```python
import feedparser
import sys

print ("Command line is : " +
str(sys.argv))

def print_item_info (target_item):
    print (target_item.title + "(" +
target_item.link + ")")

print ("Hello, world!")

feed_file = open('feeds.txt', 'r')
for this_feed in feed_file:
    print(this_feed, end="")
    print("\n\n\n")

    feed_url = this_feed

    print ("We're going to output the
feed at: " + feed_url)

    the_feed_object =
feedparser.parse(feed_url)
```

```
        print (the_feed_object.feed.title + "
was last updated " +
the_feed_object.feed.updated)

        items = the_feed_object.entries
        number_of_items = len(items)

        print ("There are {a}
items.".format(a = number_of_items))

        for this_item in items :
                print_item_info (this_item)

    feed_file.close ()
```

Now, you'll notice that all we did was indent what we
already had, and now it's part of that loop, but that we want
to close the file outside of the loop, when it's finished, so we
didn't indent that part.

```
We're going to output the feed at: https://www.cncf.io/feed

Cloud Native Computing Foundation was last updated Wed, 07 Mar 2018 19:45:23 +00
00
There are 10 items.
CNCF Sponsors New FREE "Kubernetes Deployment and Security Patterns" eBook From
The New Stack(https://www.cncf.io/blog/2018/03/07/cncf-sponsors-new-free-kuberne
tes-deployment-and-security-patterns-ebook-from-the-new-stack/)
CloudTech: "Kubernetes takes step up as it 'graduates' from Cloud Native Computi
ng Foundation"(https://www.cncf.io/news/2018/03/06/cloudtech-kubernetes-takes-st
ep-up-as-it-graduates-from-cloud-native-computing-foundation/)
Forbes: "Kubernetes Becomes The First Project To Graduate From The Cloud Native
Computing Foundation"(https://www.cncf.io/news/2018/03/06/forbes-kubernetes-beco
mes-the-first-project-to-graduate-from-the-cloud-native-computing-foundation/)
ZDNet: "Kubernetes graduates to full-pledged, open-source program"(https://www.c
ncf.io/news/2018/03/06/zdnet-%e2%80%8bkubernetes-graduates-to-full-pledged-open-
source-program/)
SD Times: "Kubernetes graduates from the Cloud Native Computing Foundation"(http
s://www.cncf.io/news/2018/03/06/sd-times-kubernetes-graduates-from-the-cloud-nat
ive-computing-foundation/)
GeekWire: "Graduation day: Kubernetes hits key milestone as CNCF lays out a clou
d-native road map"(https://www.cncf.io/news/2018/03/06/geekwire-graduation-day-k
ubernetes-hits-key-milestone-as-cncf-lays-out-a-cloud-native-road-map/)
Kubernetes Is First CNCF Project To Graduate(https://www.cncf.io/blog/2018/03/06
/kubernetes-first-cncf-project-graduate/)
```

Pretty convenient, eh? I told you, those indents are really important!

So now that we're reading all of these feeds, we can write them out to a file. We'll do that next.

Writing to a file with Python

Our last task is to take the information we're getting from these feeds and output it to a file instead of (or in addition to) the screen. To do that, we're going to open a file, just as we did before, but we're going to change the mode:

```
...
feed_file = open('feeds.txt', 'r')
item_file = open('items.txt', 'w')
...
feed_file.close()
item_file.close()
```

When we open `items.txt` as `item_file`, we're giving it a mode of `'w'`, or "write". This means that every time we run this script, the file will get wiped out and started fresh. If you wanted to just add to the end of any existing content in the file, you would use `'a'` for "append".

Notice that in order to change what we're doing, we simply added the `item_file.write()` function to the `print_item_info()` function; I told you it'd come in handy!

Now if you run the script, you'll see that you not only get the output on the screen, you also have a new text file called `items.txt` that includes just the titles of each item.

Some things to know about reading and writing files:

1) Setting the mode when opening the file determines how Python will treat that file; be very careful with `'w'`, as it will wipe out the file every time you run the script. If you don't need to write to it, set it to `'r'`; if you need to add to it, use `'a'`.

2) The `readline()` function returns the next line of the file as long as there is one, then it returns `false`. This is handy when you want to use it in a `for-loop`, as in:

```
for this_line in my_file.readline():
        print(this_line)
```

3) The `read()` function returns the entire contents of the file.

4) Make sure to close the file when you're done with it. You won't get an error if you don't -- until you try and open it again. (You can also create memory leaks by leaving files open.)

5) The `write()` function does not put each item on a new line, so if you want a newline character (`"\n"`) you will need to add it yourself.

Where to go from here

This short book just covers the very basics of working with Python. There's so much more you can do! For example, there are libraries that make it simple to create graphs and charts, or images, or work with comma-separated-values as though they were databases, or work with actual databases for that matter. As time goes by, I'll add these new features to this book, so if you want free updates, please join me at http://www.technologyformeremortals.com/python-book.

You can also check out these resources to get you going:

- The official Python documentation provides function names and parameters if you know what you're looking for, as well as howtos on various topics: https://docs.python.org/3/
- With the importance of formatting, you might want to check out PyLint (https://www.pylint.org/) and that project's style guide: https://docs.pylint.org/en/1.6.0/tutorial.html
- Tutorials Point Python Tutorial provides easy looks at various Python functions: https://www.tutorialspoint.com/python/index.htm

- *Machine Learning for Mere Mortals* gives you a look at using Python to create applications using Tensorflow: https://www.manning.com/livevideo/machine-learning-for-mere-mortals
- *Exploring Python Basics* shows you how to use Python with a Rasberry Pi: https://www.manning.com/books/exploring-python-basics

A Little Request

Thanks for sticking with me until the end! I hope you enjoyed it as much as I did. I'll be updating this book regularly, so please go ahead and leave me your email address so I can send you the updated versions as they're published by joining me at http://bit.ly/2JsSQn9.

If you've enjoyed this book, please do me a solid and leave an honest review at Amazon (https://amzn.to/2WVWIAi). It really helps.

Thanks, and I hope to see you next time!